AZIZ ANSARI

HEATHER MOORE NIVER

THE
GIANTS
OF COMEDY™

AZIZ ANSARI

HEATHER MOORE NIVER

ROSEN
PUBLISHING

Published in 2016 by The Rosen Publishing Group, Inc.
29 East 21st Street, New York, NY 10010

First Edition

Library of Congress Cataloging-in-Publication Data

Niver, Heather Moore.
 Aziz Ansari / Heather Moore Niver. — First edition.
     pages cm. — (The giants of comedy)
 Includes bibliographical references and index.
 ISBN 978-1-5081-7051-8 (library bound)
 1. Ansari, Aziz, 1983—Juvenile literature. 2. Actors—United
States—Biography—Juvenile literature. 3. Comedians—United States—
Biography—Juvenile literature. I. Title.
 PN2287.A65N58 2015
 791.4502'8092—dc23
 [B]

                                                    2015025512

Manufactured in China

CONTENTS

INTRODUCTION

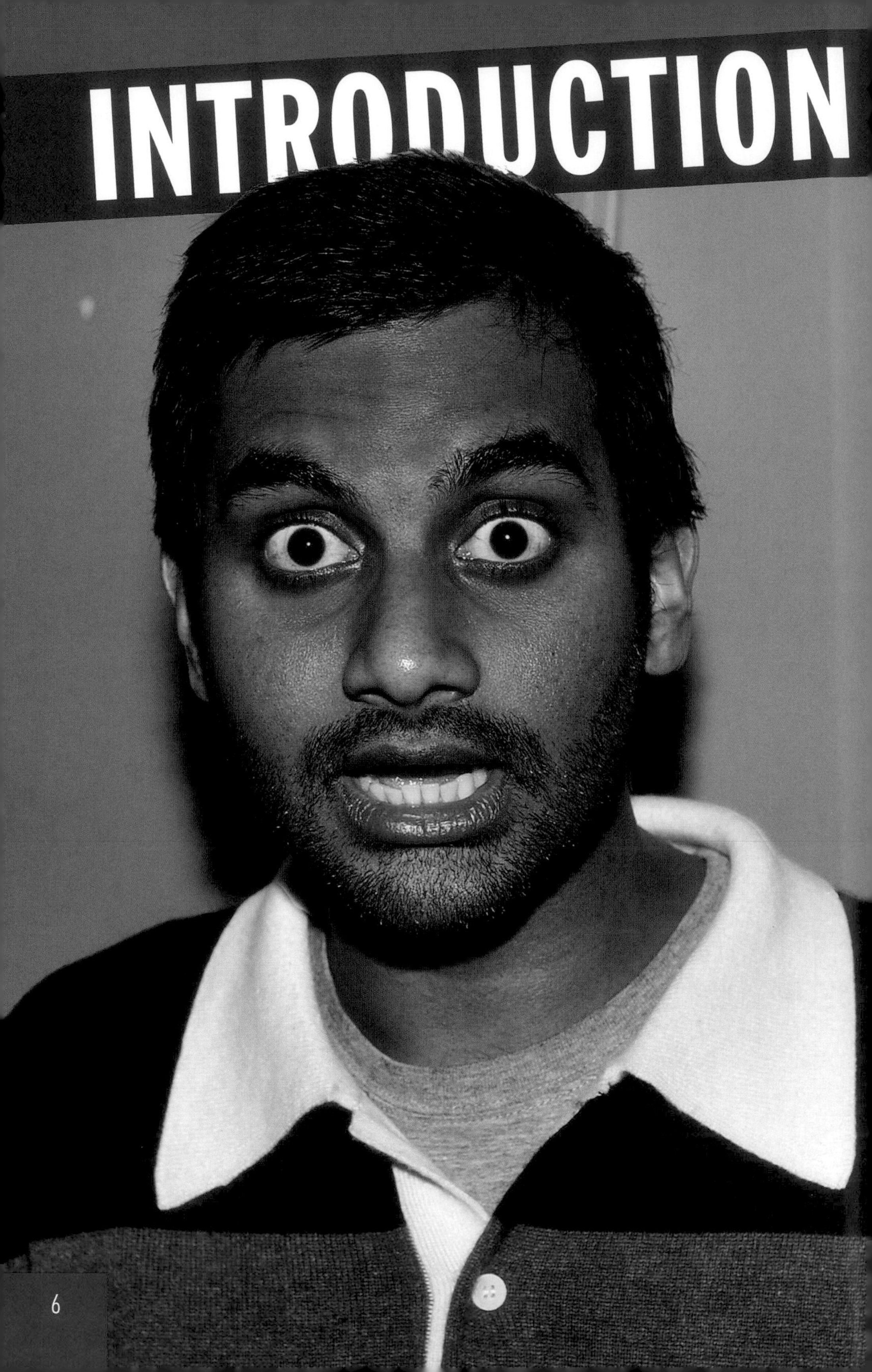

A

ziz Ansari is a comedian for our times. As comedy star Chris Rock told New York Times reporter Dave Itzkoff, "in this weird, brownish-beige, mixed-up, what-is-your-nationality world we're starting to live in, who is better than Aziz to be the new Jerry Seinfeld?" That's not a bad recommendation from a comedy legend who just happens to have been one of Aziz Ansari's earliest role models and comedic inspirations. Ansari became interested in comedy at a young age and started working at it during college at open-mike nights. Almost immediately after graduation, this smart and funny young man practically bolted into the spotlight.

Ansari's good fortune in his faster-than-the-speed-of-light rise to fame is not lost on him. He started out performing in rock clubs, put out his first special, and soon he was splitting sides with laughter in theaters everywhere, even Carnegie Hall and Madison Square Garden. But his success doesn't

In a relatively short amount of time, Aziz Ansari has crafted his own niche of comedy that has people both thinking and rolling in the aisles.

seem to have changed his work ethic: keep doing the work and keep improving his performances and jokes and everything will take care of itself.

A one-hour comedy show takes months to cultivate and perfect. How does Ansari know when his show is ready? Well, he takes it to a live audience and tries out his jokes. It's a risky way to refine a routine, but he immediately knows which jokes work because they get resounding laughs.

It would be easy to write Ansari off as a young jokester, but he takes his work, and all comedy, seriously. He thinks it should get more respect. As he explained to Carrie Battan in an article for the website *Pitchfork*, "You should really treat stand-up like you would a … one-man play. It bums me out that people don't really respect it as an art." In England, comedy acts are reviewed alongside plays. He commented that the English reviews for his special *Dangerously Delicious* were "very thoughtful," whereas American reviewers "usually come and take three jokes and misquote them." Ansari hopes that Americans will approach comedy a little more seriously someday.

He also sees a lack of respect during his own performances in the United States. "If you're in a comedy club here, people are eating wings…texting," he told Battan. "If you went to a play, no one would be texting during the show. Every show I do, someone at some point starts texting, even after I make a scene about it, saying, 'Please don't do it, I'm begging you. It's distracting, please don't.'" But Ansari explains that his disapproval goes beyond mere manners. It wreaks havoc with the routine he has spent months developing. "If you're sitting there flashing a thing in my face, that's gonna distract me. Stand-up has rhythms, it's like a performance."

Aziz Ansari is not your everyday comedian. He has a unique perspective that has audiences clutching their sides with laughter all over the world. Although some aspects of his work might raise eyebrows—such as his crude language, explicit sexual descriptions, and the infamous Rude Randy character—Ansari's thoughtful yet hilarious insights have people watching to see where this young Indian-American comedian will go next.

CHAPTER ONE

From a Small Town to the Big Time

Aziz Ansari has come a long way since his childhood in Bennettsville, South Carolina. He was a smart, funny child, and he has matured into a smarter and even funnier adult, one who is always studying the quirky nuances of American culture and human behavior.

Young Blood

Aziz Ansari's parents are from Tamil Nadu, India, which means that Ansari is of Tamil Indian heritage. But Ansari called Bennettsville, South Carolina, home when he was a boy. He was born on February 23, 1983, in Columbia, South

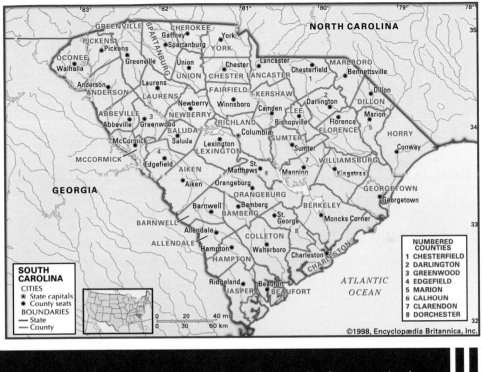

Although Aziz Ansari's parents are from India, he was raised in Bennettsville, South Carolina. In school, he was a smart and funny kid.

Carolina, to Shoukath and Fatima Ansari. His mom, Fatima, works in the medical office where his dad, Shoukath, is a gastroenterologist.

His name leads many people to conclude that Ansari is a Muslim—Aziz is usually a Muslim name, and Ansari is almost always one. That makes it unsurprising to learn that Shoukath and Fatima Ansari are indeed Muslim. However, while their son is sometimes described as following the Muslim faith, a *New York Times* article by Dave Itzkoff clarifies that Aziz Ansari considers himself an atheist. He doesn't believe in any god.

Ansari doesn't have many stories about the struggles of growing up as a person of Indian heritage in South Carolina. "Most of the time it was pretty fine," he told journalist and music critic Kelefa Sanneh about grade school. Pretty early on, it was clear the school had someone special on their hands. Young Aziz only spent a few months in first grade before he was promoted to second, and all the kids noticed. "It was just, like, 'Who is this little brown kid? He's a genius!'" He told radio host Terry Gross, "I never saw an Indian person on TV unless it was like Gandhi or a James Bond movie where he goes to India or they're showing the Kwik-E-Mart guy. There was no one Indian on TV."

From first grade through tenth grade, Aziz Ansari went to an independent school called Marlboro Academy. Because the school was so small, there were only about twenty kids in his class. As he grew up—in the days before the Internet—Aziz and his classmates had to entertain one another. Their town didn't have concerts or even a movie theater. In high school, he taught himself how to play the guitar and listened to bands like Led Zeppelin and Metallica. Ansari was interested in other people and different ways of living from a young age. "Even just meeting kids from different parts of South Carolina kind of expanded my exposure to different cultural things. So that increased my interest in different things," he told Gross. So began a lifelong interest in observing people, places, and things.

For his junior year of high school, Aziz moved on to South Carolina Governor's School for Science and Mathematics (GSSM) in Hartsville. GSSM is a school for students from across the state who are interested in math and science. Even though he was known as a funny guy, Aziz was also a tennis star and got excellent grades. He's remembered at the school as being one of the smart kids who wanted to sit in the front of the classroom, although sitting in front wasn't so unusual at GSSM.

During the summer of his junior year, he worked on a research project about the body's ability to fight off disease, or immunology. He enjoyed it, but realized science wasn't his calling. He told *Charleston City Paper's* Susan Cohen, "After a while I just decided 'All right. I know enough about cells. This is getting too abstract and intangible.'" Naturally, he was already developing his own sense of humor. Sometimes his sense of humor was even a little geeky, like the summer he and a friend decided to read their entire biology textbook for summer reading.

EARLY IDOLS

When Ansari was in high school, he saw his first Chris Rock comedy specials. For Ansari, the timing was perfect because they really got the young funnyman interested in stand up. (He also loved—and still loves—Eddie Murphy's *Delirious* and *Coming to America.*) In an article on Ansari's 2015 Madison Square Garden performance, *New York Times* reporter Jason Zinoman noticed a few bits in which Rock's influence on Ansari was particularly notable: "The one foot stomping, the defiantly repeated phrases that sound almost like incantations, the ferocious pacing—Mr. Ansari has clearly studied his Chris Rock."

Ansari's early influences—who include the comedians Louis C.K. and Patton Oswalt alongside Rock—are still evident in his hard work. "All the best have a tremendous work ethic," he told Jay Richardson in an interview for the website *Chortle.* These comedians constantly rewrite their routines from the beginning. And they do shows over and over, working out their routines and jokes until they get them right. In Ansari's opinion, all the best comics perform all the time.

Once during college, Ansari was in the audience on a night when Rock dropped in to try out some material. This experience had a lasting influence. He saw that some of Rock's material wasn't necessarily getting laughs, but that the celebrity didn't let it bother him. He just went on to another joke.

College-Bound for Comedy

In 2000, Ansari left South Carolina to head to college at New York University's Stern School of Business. He started out his college career majoring in marketing, but soon after he got there, he realized it wasn't a good fit. Although he considered switching majors and going to NYU's Tisch School of the Arts, he never got around to making the move.

Almost as soon as Ansari arrived at college, he started performing at local open-mike nights, telling stories. "I was 18 when I started. I was hanging out with some friends and they asked if I had tried stand-up before. I hadn't, but I thought: 'What the hell?' So I went to an open-mic night, and I liked it," he told Jessica Hundley in an interview for the website *AskMen*. Ansari would hand out promotional flyers for the club on the weekends in exchange for time on stage. Although he admits it was terrifying to be up on stage at first, the laughs meant more. He quickly became more comfortable on stage and kept working on his material.

The audiences at one theater, Upright Citizens Brigade (UCB) Theatre, loved him. Amy Poehler, the successful comedian from *Saturday Night Live* who went on to star with Ansari in *Parks and Recreation*, said that before she met Ansari, she heard that he was selling out shows on Tuesdays at midnight.

Matt Besser, Amy Poehler, Ian Roberts, and Matt Walsh founded the Upright Citizens Brigade, where Ansari started selling out shows on Tuesdays, typically a slow night.

Trading in a Business Suit for a Microphone

Shortly after gradu-
ation, Ansari started
hosting a comedy
night known as
Human Giant at the
UCB with two estab-
lished funny guys,
Rob Huebel and Paul
Scheer. He told jour-
nalist Hundley, "With
Human Giant, we were
writing and perform-
ing and producing
every show. It's a lot
of work—fun—but a
lot of work." In 2005,
they decided to put
Human Giant on film,
hiring Jason Woliner
as director. They
filmed a number of
shorts, which fell into the hands of MTV executive
Tony DiSanto. He liked it enough to offer them a
pilot, which led to broadcast for two seasons. In one

ON THE JOB

Like many students, Ansari worked while he took classes. During college, he had a job working for NYU's Heating Ventilation and Air Conditioning Department. He also told the arts and culture magazine *Blackbook*, "I was a dishwasher at one of those Japanese places that cook on your table. Not too fun."

Ansari never talked to his parents about trading in his business suit for a microphone. But, by the time he graduated with a bachelor's degree in marketing in 2004, Ansari was already working regularly and successfully as a stand-up comic. He told journalist Aimee Groth, "When I graduated, I just kept doing stand-up and never did anything with my degree. Getting a marketing degree at NYU was an expensive but easy way to procrastinate having to find a real job while I figured out how to make a career as a comedian."

Ansari did work for an Internet advertising business after college, but it wasn't long before he decided he was making enough money doing stand-up comedy that he could stop working for the web. Thanks to his connections with Upright Citizens Brigade, he scored steady work as an emcee of a weekly stand-up showcase called *Crash Test* at the UCB Theatre.

episode, after hitting a deer with his car, Ansari is forced to dress up like a shrub for a week. In another, he plays a police officer who pursues criminals by hot air balloon. *Human Giant* was popular, but Ansari and his partners decided not to do a third season, mainly because all the guys wanted to work on some of their own projects.

Paul Scheer and Rob Huebel worked with Ansari on both the *Human Giant* comedy night and the MTV show.

Human Giant turned out to be Ansari's first acting experience. The more experiences he had with acting, the better he got. He told Richardson, "For me, *Human Giant* was like how other people have *Saturday Night Live* as their training ground. It was my college." Later, when he was hired to work on the television show *Parks and Recreation*, he had plenty of acting experience under his belt. He was ready.

Parks and Recreation

In 2008, after the end of *Human Giant*, Ansari moved to Los Angeles, California, and within a few months scored a role in the movie *Funny People* (with Adam Sandler and Seth Rogan) and was offered the role of Tom Haverford in the mock-documentary television show *Parks and Recreation*. In fact, the producers hired Ansari to work on *Parks and Recreation* before its *Saturday Night Live* star Amy Poehler was cast as the main character or they even had a concrete vision for the television show. The show's creator, Michael Schur, described Ansari to Itzkoff as both sarcastic and loveable. "He defies categorization… There's so much going on with him that we felt it would be funny just to have him and Amy Poehler in the same room." Ansari didn't have to be asked twice to be involved with the show. "They could've told me the premise is that you and Vin Diesel run a day-care center together and at night you fight crime, and it's shot like 'The Office,' documentary-style," Ansari told *Wall Street Journal* reporter Ellen Gamerman. "I'd be like, 'I'm doing that show.'"

Ansari became popular as the character Tom Haverford, the well-dressed and ambitious administrator (and womanizer) in all seven seasons of the show. Although most of his stand-up material revolves around personal experiences, Ansari says

Ansari, far right, poses with the *Parks and Recreation* cast. He performed as the smartly dressed Tom Haverford in all seven seasons of the show.

he doesn't have a lot in common with his character. They both have a fascination with nice suits and like hip hop music, but that's where the similarities end.

Parks and Recreation wasn't a hit right from the start. The show didn't premiere until the middle of the season and episodes were cut. But Schur was confident. Ansari told entertainer Chris Hardwick that Schur never lost hope. He remembered him telling the cast, "Let's just have a really funny show and everything else will take care of itself." And obviously, it did. The show became a huge critical hit.

In 2009, Ansari also appeared in several episodes of the television show *Scrubs* as an all-too-casual medical intern who makes staff and patients very uncomfortable. But his character's appearance was only to last for a handful of episodes. Almost as soon as Ansari was cast in *Parks and Recreation*, he was written off *Scrubs* for good.

In general, *Parks and Recreation* involves almost no ad-lib material. However, producer Dean Holland told Sanneh that he gave the camera operators strict instructions: "Once Aziz starts going on all of his ad libs, stick with him." He reportedly improvised a line in which he convinces Poehler, who has had too much to drink, to fax a fruit snack. As Poehler explained to writer Melia Robinson, they would do one last take, or "fun run," for each scene to let the actors improvise. Most of the time, the lines weren't used in the final show, "But it made the actors feel funny. It kept the crew laughing and on their toes."

Ansari told Hundley that *Parks and Recreation* was "the easiest job I've ever had." He says the writers were open and funny. "I come in and I act and then I go to my trailer and have a chicken salad and watch *Breaking Bad* on DVD."

Over the years, Ansari's voice has been featured in animated films and television. His vocal talents

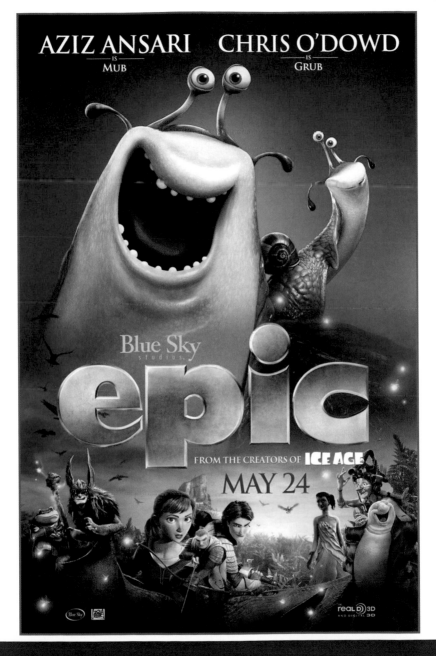

Aziz Ansari has both performed in movies and provided hilarious character voices in animated films. In Blue Sky's *Epic*, he performed as the voice of Mub the slug.

are regularly featured on Fox's animated television show *Bob's Burgers* as the nerdy character Darryl. Some of his other more popular voice roles have included characters in animated films, such as a slug (Mub) in *Epic* and a rabbit (Squint) in *Ice Age: Continental Drift.*

Post-*Parks* Life and Funny Nonfiction

In April 2015, as *Parks and Recreation* came to an end, Ansari wasn't about to take a break. On his Tumblr page "Ansari Is Bored," he reported that he was already filming an original series with his *Parks and Recreation* "buds" Alan Yang and Mike Schur for the online streaming company Netflix. Although at first the premise wasn't announced, it later emerged that it would be called *Master of None* and would focus on a young actor—played by Ansari—living in New York. Other funny cast members, such as Eric Wareheim, H. Jon Benjamin, Kevin Yu, and Lena Waithe, were announced. Actress Claire Daines was also on board to contribute her talents to the series.

In 2013, Ansari got his first book deal (reportedly for a whopping $3.5 million) with Penguin Press, which was published and in bookstores all over the world in June 2015. In his book, titled *Modern Romance*, Ansari writes about relationships—notably, communication in such a technological age. He

In 2015, Ansari published his first book, *Modern Romance*, a funny yet informative book about the quirks and issues of today's relationships.

told *Daily Beast* reporter Abby Haglage that he got the idea when he was doing research on modern relationships. "When I was researching what it's like to find love in this modern area, trying to find articles about this stuff, I was like: why isn't there a[n] … analysis about this stuff that exists? And then I was like, OH MAN, I should write that book!" So he did. Ansari set out to write a book that was funny but interesting. He also saw it as a chance to do some things he can't do in stand up. Ansari worked with sociologists and other academics to come up with experiments for his book.

CHAPTER TWO

On the Stage and Between the Pages

Ansari has practically rocketed to fame and is listed among the funniest comedians out there, despite his relatively young age. He joins the ranks of stand-up comedians such as Louis C.K., mixing up his shows by performing at theaters as well as arenas, including Madison Square Garden.

Getting Cozy With Aziz

Although his first two specials were criticized for being a bit chaotic and lacking organization, Ansari's infectious enthusiasm for his subjects carried them through. In 2010 Ansari performed his first special, *Intimate Moments for a Sensual Evening*. He was just twenty-six years old, so it is made up of material he wrote when he was in his early-to-mid twenties. This film-length

Ansari poses with actor and rapper RZA at the *Funny People* premier. Ansari's first special is full of jokes about rappers and his memorably rude "RAAAAAAAANDY" character.

special (146 minutes) is chock-full of lively stories about "hanging out with famous rappers," such as Kanye West. In the final ten minutes, he comes out as his *Funny People* character Randy, complete with gaudy, flashy suit, dancers, a DJ, and even a smoke machine.

Intimate Moments for a Sensual Evening is a good introduction to Ansari's early work. Hailed for his crossover abilities, Ansari is as at home talking about indie rock as he is joking about rap. In a review for *Pitchfork*, Ian Cohen wrote, "It's pop smarts that define Ansari's performance: He's relatable without pandering and clever without making a flex of intellect or being overly arch." Even a few years later, he is still proud of this work. He explained to comedy journalist Elise Czajkowski, "People definitely become better comedians. I think it's good, I still stand by it, but I definitely think I'm a much better comedian than I was when I did those other specials, and I hope that I continue to get better." This is a theme that has continued throughout his career. Aziz Ansari is always trying to improve his game.

A Delicious Taste of Comedy

Almost three years later, he presented eager fans with *Dangerously Delicious*. With this special, Ansari starts to tackle more grown-up and universal topics, like love, marriage, and having babies. He explained to Terry Gross, "I see a lot of my friends are kind of entering serious stages of their lives where they're getting married and having children, and I'm getting to the age where that stuff is getting expected of me and it's all very terrifying to me." It is also full of familiar topics, such as R. Kelly, Ansari's cousin Harris, and trouble with girls, making *Dangerously Delicious* a little too much like a continuation of *Intimate Moments* for some critics. He does get more personal with the audience this time around, however, especially when talking about his own experiences in the dating world. And he goes into more detail on some subjects, too, describing and acting out some possibly blush-inducing things that are not for the faint of heart. Fortunately, he holds back from being an all-out crude comic in this special.

RUDE, RAUNCHY, AND RAAAAAAAANDY

Ansari might be very focused on making his routines and specials "undeniably good," but that doesn't stop him from joking about what some may consider rude and even offensive subjects or from using some rough language. Ansari became well known for his character

"Raaaaaaaandy" (his name eventually evolved to be spelled and pronounced with eight As), in Judd Apatow's 2009 film *Funny People*. Randy is rude, raunchy, and has a pretty filthy vocabulary. Those who are familiar with Ansari's comedy will know that he is not the least bit shy about using expletives. Although Randy's jokes are Ansari's jokes, as Randy the punch lines are far filthier and the language is a lot coarser, to put it mildly. Ansari refers to plenty of sex in his comedy, but Randy gets downright vulgar. Kelefa Sanneh suggests that Randy's crass character was created "to represent everything that was wrong with stand-up comedy." Randy's jokes always go for a laugh by way of a curse word rather than a punch line. Ansari feels his challenge is to keep his audiences laughing at Randy and his profanities, not with him.

The very randy Randy character was just a small part in the movie, but he has become wildly popular among other comedians (such as Seth Rogan, who performed in *Funny People* as well) and audiences alike. A website was created for Randy, and Apatow even funded Ansari's three-part documentary about the crude comedian, in which Randy is geeky, but just as gross. For example, Randy enjoys superimposing his head onto the bodies of porn stars.

It's a fine line between Ansari's comedy and his character. "He's afraid it will eventually destroy him," Amy Poehler joked—mostly—to Sanneh. "I think he fights to make sure that people don't think that's actually him. Which it certainly isn't." Over the years, Ansari has performed segments of his shows as Randy, but sometimes he declines requests, joking that Randy has died.

Comedy Six Feet Under

In 2013, Ansari brought out his *Buried Alive* performance. This time, he changed his tactic and offered his audiences a more personal show, discussing his feelings as his friends coupled up and had children and as he eased into a new decade of life: his thirties. *Buried Alive* tackles more than simple dating; Ansari covers equality in marriage and social graces, as well as how smartphones have changed romance. The special includes some of his trademark observations, but this time, his observations are so intuitive that critics noticed how they set him apart from an average comedian. Erik Adams, writing a review for the *A.V. Club*, described it as "craftsmanship... The crowd work portions of the set are off-the-cuff, but like any worthwhile work of improvised comedy, they land because Ansari is so practiced and so disciplined...I love the beat he takes after the couple near the front of the stage inserts a basket of breadsticks into their engagement story. He pounces immediately, but then steps back before asking if the breadsticks were unlimited. It's a one-time-only routine with a seasoned execution."

It's probably no surprise that in a special called *Buried Alive,* when Ansari starts talking about relationships, he focuses on the "'til death"

Ansari stops for photos, in a snappy suit, of course, at his 2013 *Buried Alive* premiere. In this special, he gets up-close and personal with his audience.

aspect—especially with marriage. He looks at the darker side of the symbols and oaths of marriage, which seem much creepier when presented in a different context. Try not to shiver when Ansari presents questions such as these as if from the lips of a psychopath: "Will you spend the rest of your life with me?" "Will you wear this symbol of our love on your finger?" In this special, Ansari is curious and quizzical, bringing up observations about all the crazy things people do. He offers questions and presents his research, all while keeping his audience in stitches.

Live at the Garden

In October 2014, Ansari not only performed at Madison Square Garden but also joined an impressive—and impressively short—list of comedians who have sold out the venue: Eddie Murphy, George Carlin, Andrew Dice Clay, Chris Rock, Russell Peters, Dane Cook, Kevin Hart, and Louis C.K. For some reason, Madison Square Garden doesn't play host to all that many comedians. Nevertheless, its vice president, Bob Shea, told Dave Itzkoff that they were eager for Ansari to perform there, because "he's a star across many different entertainment platforms."

Concerned that a stand-up comedy show at such a massive venue could be visually

His Madison Square Garden gig was a very big deal for Ansari, who knew that only a handful of comedians had performed their material there.

uninteresting, Ansari went beyond the usual to arrange for a huge screen above him as he performed. He told journalist Jesse David Fox in an interview for *New York Magazine's Vulture* website, "So wherever I'm walking, there's a guy shooting me head-to-toe, and it never cuts. Wherever I walk, there's a giant Aziz above me. Then people are actually looking at me, at my eyeline, and I can feel them looking at me. I've done other shows… and on those, they just have two screens on the right and left, and everybody is watching the screen." Instead of a room full of people watching a special, they're all still looking at the performer. He filmed the show and called it *Aziz Ansari: Live at Madison Square Garden*.

At Madison Square Garden, Ansari slowed down his routine with much longer stories than in his previous specials. Although Jason Zinoman called it his most ambitious work, he also referred to it as Ansari's least funny special so far. In an article describing the special in the *Atlantic* magazine, though, David Sims wrote, "It's always impressive when a stand-up can command a crowd with quieter material, but it's particularly impressive when it's happening in a colossal, sold-out venue."

Between the Pages

"Hello, I'm Aziz Ansari. Comedian, actor, lover of tacos and fine TV dramas, and now author!" And so he introduces his book on his website. In 2013, Ansari was offered the opportunity to write a book, but he wasn't about to add any old title to the shelves of celebrity memoirs. According to Melia Robinson, Ansari explained, "You know when you text someone you're romantically interested in and you don't hear anything back and then you see them post a photo of a pizza on Instagram? That's exactly what I want this to deal with."

With an impressive $3.5 million paycheck attached to the project, the quippy comedian wrote a book he hoped would be as awesome as it was academic. On his website he introduces the book like this: "But the transformation of our romantic lives cannot be explained by technology alone…In a short period of time, the whole culture of finding love and a mate has changed dramatically. A few decades ago, people would find a decent person who lived in their neighborhood. Their families would meet and, after deciding neither party seemed like a murderer, in about six months, the new couple would get married and soon have a kid, all by the time they were twenty-four. Today, people marry later than ever and spend years of their lives on a quest to find the perfect person, a soulmate." So he teamed up with New York University professor and sociologist Eric Klinenberg to write and research *Modern Romance*. Ansari developed a full research project, did countless interviews with people of all ages from all over the world, conducted focus groups, and consulted social scientists as well.

To complement his research, and true to his performances, Ansari reached out to his fans by polling them on a website he set up, called *Modern*

When writing *Modern Romance*, Ansari collaborated with NYU's Eric Klinenberg. Together, they researched contemporary love, even creating a website where people could weigh in on their experiences.

Romantics. There he asked questions such as how dating in the smartphone age had changed being single. He asked for people's feedback about using newspaper classifieds to get dates and whether or not (and why or why not) they had engaged in sexting. More than five thousand readers and contributors followed the page, answering questions from the comedian, knowing full well that their answers could be published in his finished book.

Ansari bantered with and answered the people who posted to his page, weighing the pros and cons of technology's role in dating. When a painfully shy user told the story of using Facebook as way to start chatting with a girl he'd just met, Ansari replied, "THIS is the kind of story that gets lost too often in these discussions. The notion that tends to get most play is that all this technology is keeping us less present and ultimately more disconnected and flakey—while I think this is valid and true to a large extent—in the book we don't want to forget this stuff. Social media gave you a tool to overcome your shyness and meet someone. Cool." Readers can expect a book that's interesting, informative, and, of course, hilarious.

CHAPTER **THREE**

Being Undeniably Good

As he told Chris Hardwick, Ansari has one main goal. It is, in the words of comedy legend Steve Martin, "Be undeniably good." He takes that quote to heart, and he offers it up to young comedians who feel like they're not getting credit for their talent. He recognizes the difficulty of being in that position, but points out that none of the great comedians point to the day they e-mailed a famous comedian for advice, crediting it for making them who they are today.

Honing your comedic talent can be hard, frustrating work, but Ansari suggests that comedians who are just starting out keep doing their work and trying to get better. And when they do get better, they should keep working on getting even better than that. Eventually, their work may shake things up and get them noticed, whereas the angry resentful people are so focused on their negative feelings that they just fade away. People who work hard and push through are the ones Ansari thinks do great work and pique interest.

Ansari told Hardwick that he believes that comedians—or any kind of artists for that matter—need to be "incredibly talented, incredibly lucky, and incredibly smart… And incredibly nice. You gotta be cool." In fact, Ansari remembers that when they were casting

Ansari clowns around with his costar Amy Poehler, whom he has described as one of the nicest people he knows.

for *Human Giant*, they would turn applicants away if they acted like jerks. He goes on to question if it is any coincidence that Amy Poehler and Will Ferrell are the coolest, nicest people? No, he says. Comedy shows like *Parks and Recreation* don't happen with just one person; they need a team for support in all kinds of ways. People love working on the show in large part because Poehler is one of the nicest people in the business. No one would want to work with her—no matter how great the show—if she was a nasty boss.

Crafting Comedy

When he was first getting started, Ansari would think of funny things to talk about that would make the audience laugh. As he's become more experienced and a bit older, he's thinking more about interesting subjects to tackle. At the same time, his topics are more personal areas of life that he admits he wasn't comfortable talking about when he was younger, such as love, marriage, and having children. "Oh, this is my life. I'm an adult now. Whatever it is," he joked to Jesse David Fox.

Preparing a comedy show is a lot more work than people may think. It is far more than lounging around, thinking up the number of quips, funny stories, or jokes that will fill an hour with laughs. Perhaps some comedians work that way, but Aziz Ansari takes his comedy specials and shows very seriously. He spent the entire summer before his now-famous Madison Square Garden show in preparation. "You have to be the one to come up with it," he told Dave Itzkoff. "There's no magic person that's like 'You should do this.' It's on you to figure this out." And he does.

Jockeying for Jokes

In his early thirties, Ansari's starting point is with research. That sounds serious, but he works his research into some sidesplitting comedy. He begins by gathering different ideas and when he hits on what he thinks is a good idea, he delves into the information. He explained to Dave Itzkoff that he starts out with "the things that really consume your head, the ideas that are really deep down," and then he works out the funniest way to talk about them.

Relationships were a big topic in his *Modern Romance* and *Buried Alive* specials. As he prepared the special that would become *Modern Romance*, he started out by reading books, scientific articles, and research about dating. As he explained to Hardwick, his approach boils down to taking "very smart people's ideas and…applying them to whatever I'm talking about." For example, one article he read questioned whether or not the vast choices people have in choosing with whom to have a relationship is actually overwhelming. Perhaps so many dating options instead works against finding a good mate. One study that showed that having more choices turns out to be more stressful and less satisfying in the long run. This was an interesting starting point for Ansari to start writing jokes for *Modern Romance*.

PASSION FOR POP

One of Ansari's tactics is to approach some of the culture's more outrageous behaviors with what Kelefa Sanneh calls "half-crazed wonder" instead of mocking them like most comedians do. For example, in 2010, he decided to cave and watch the movie *Twilight*, all the while tweeting his reactions. "'Dude is a vampire! Did NOT see this coming.'" But don't think that Ansari is overly positive. He just thinks that reveling in this absurd society is more interesting than outright bashing it.

He loves the little oddities of pop culture, too, and that sets Ansari apart from many other comedians. For example, in one stand-up routine, he talks about how he thinks he will come to his end as a result of his obsession with popular culture: "Comedian Aziz Ansari was killed in a car accident today. He was struck by another vehicle while using IMDb to see if Val Kilmer was, indeed, in the film 'Willow.'"

Because he likes his routines and specials to revolve around themes, sometimes he works up hilarious jokes that don't quite fit in with his topics. Bits that don't work with the theme may get worked into an encore, such as a bit about going out for ice cream that was an encore for a *Buried Alive* show that focused on marriage and love and dating.

Aziz Ansari, shown here in 2010, likes to work out material in front of a live audience. He also records these shows so he can critique them later.

Sampling on Stage

For Aziz, a major part of refining his jokes and rou- tines occurs in front of a live audience. To start out, he prepares what amount to notes, or basic bullet points about what he wants to discuss on stage. As he tries them out for a crowd, he records his improvisations to listen to and think about later. "That's why you tour it so much, so you're sure you have the best joke," he explained to Hardwick. When a joke or story doesn't get the laugh he expected, he makes a note of it and thinks about different and funnier ways to approach it. He told Jay Richardson, "It's a lot of repetition and refinement. Yesterday I started my first show at 8pm, then did my last at midnight. It took three shows to figure out how to make the jokes better…I'd rather it was a year and a half before I put out a special and have it be great, than a year and it not be so good." Every audience is a new focus group, helping him figure out what works (when they laugh) and what doesn't (when an awkward silence hangs over the room).

Trying it Live

One of the coolest things about fame for Ansari is dropping in at comedy clubs. He remembers being in a New York club and seeing Chris Rock just drop in. At some point, comedians become so well known that they can drop in wherever they want to try out new material. This is a treat for the lucky audience in whatever club a comedian picks. The one downside is that the comedian is likely working on new material, not all of which is the comedian's funniest work.

These days, Ansari has reached that level of popularity that he can drop into clubs in New York City and Los Angles and practice. "I even tell the audience, 'You're getting an inferior version of the

Ansari remembers seeing Chris Rock (shown here in 2014), a major comedic influence for him, drop in at a comedy club to work out jokes in front of an audience.

joke, so I can work on it myself.'" At first he finds the crowds happy and receptive and nice and cool, but that's hardly honest feedback. After a few minutes, the excitement goes down and the crowd is more realistic. In 2010, at the Upright Citizens Brigade Theatre, Itzkoff reported that Ansari told the crowd, "I know you're thinking, 'Man, this is going a little long,' I know it is. That's the goal. So I can tighten it up and make it better later." Ansari will try out different versions of the same joke on different nights until he finally finds the delivery that works, even if it takes twenty tries.

Once he has about forty-five minutes of material he likes, Ansari puts it together and does performances at smaller theaters. For example, he'll announce last-minute shows, just for the opportunity to try out his routine, or "album," in full and see how the audience reacts. Once Ansari has a full hour, he'll start performing at larger theaters, usually in cities he didn't get the chance to perform in on his last tour. Finally, when he feels like he has the complete act together, he tours big cities. When he puts together an hour of new material and shares it with new audiences on tour, he's really fulfilled.

Don't be fooled. Though he loves it, this process requires a tremendous amount of work. And he is highly amused when people expect him to be working on new material immediately after putting out an album. He commiserated with fellow comedian Hardwick, pointing out that reporters and journalists wouldn't go up to a famous director who has just finished a project—such as Christopher Nolan right after he'd made the movie *Inception*—and ask why that the director hadn't made another movie yet. Ansari points out that a comedy special is a lot like a one-person play. And coming up with a thought-provoking hour really takes a long time.

Interviewing the Audience

Ansari is hardly the first or only comedian to interact with his audience, but it is a key part of his act. In characteristic fashion, he puts a lot of thought into these interactions. He listens to a lot of interviews by radio personality Howard Stern, for example, which he likes because they're so casual. By talking to people like this, Ansari feels like he quickly forms bonds with people and can ask them about their lives. In *Buried Alive,* Ansari questions people about their marriage proposals. Every one is different, making each show that much more unique.

When he was writing *Buried Alive*, Ansari started asking audience members about online dating, something he's never done. He joked to Chris Hardwick, "I think if you're a public person you'd get murdered eventually." He uses interviews with his audience to learn intimate details he might not

Ansari often asks the audience intimate questions about their lives. But he's not so open when talking about his own life.

otherwise encounter. He also enjoys hearing about new perspectives from all different walks of life. Ansari asks people questions about whether or not they felt doubts when they got married. He told Hardwick, "it's just super interesting because you can ask these people like very personal questions on stage and they'll just answer you. They'll tell you things. And you learn a lot 'cause everyone's life story and experience is just super interesting." In one case, an audience member started talking about his parents' divorce and the misgivings that they had when they married.

Even though Ansari will grill audience members during his routine, he is reluctant to spill much in the way of specifics about his own life when asked. Ansari can be very forthright in his routines about his feeling about love, dating, and marriage, so it can feel awkward for him when he knows someone has heard all this. Ansari uses a pseudonym for almost everything, even when he does something as simple as hailing a cab using the Uber app.

Routines and Research

One thing that is always a constant with Ansari is his precise process. He has always tried to record his shows and to review the previous show before moving on to the next show. If he forgets to make a recording, he reviews it over and over in his head, trying to remember exactly how it went.

Right before a show, Ansari heads to the quiet of his trailer. He sacks out on a couch or chair and pulls out a digital recorder, huge headphones, and his notebook. He cues up the latest recording of a performance and listens to it, noting which jokes and comments got the laughs and are worth repeating. His goal is to have an hour of material that he's really excited about. That's Ansari's definition of success. He thinks it's great to be able to fill a theater, but it's more satisfying to know he's improved and developed a show that's even better than the last one.

Some of Ansari's topics might seem pretty casual and off-the-cuff—just about every comedian talks about love and dating—but it's not uncommon for him to do a lot of research on a topic. As Ansari began writing *Modern Romance,* he worked with scholars to get details and specific numbers and statistics. His *Parks and Recreation* costar Nick Offerman told journalist Amanda Dobbins, "Once he gets a bone, he is very much like an avid dog, chewing it and gleaning every bit of flavor he can from it."

In fact, when Ansari was lunching with Dobbins, the pair start talking about marriage and when people decide to do it. Dobbins points out how, for many women, their biological clock begins really ticking at age thirty (as the number of years for having a child begins to decrease). Ansari replies, "I read in the *Atlantic* that that was a false age," he says. "I should look that up." And he does. Within days he e-mails the writer the article he mentioned, even going so far as to highlight the pertinent facts.

Comedic Evolution

But no matter how nice you are, how hard you work, or how talented you are, every comedian has to think about his or her future. And for Ansari that can be scary. Sure, he knows he's popular and making a good living now, but he has a whole lot of career ahead of him. Will he have to tour for the rest of his life? He is keenly aware that in a couple of years he may not be as popular with the public and he could easily be a distant memory. So that's one reason why he's always pushing his work, trying to change it up and make it new. He runs into fans who

FUNNY FOODIE

Ansari likes food as much as he likes comedy. He likes it so much he practically gets giddy when talking about the Taco Zone taco truck and its secret off-menu items. When he's on tour he thinks of it as a food tour as much as a comedy tour. In each city he tries to sniff out lesser-known restaurants and tries new and unusual food combinations.

His friends call him their personal Yelp (a website that features restaurant and other entertainment reviews from users). When they're in a new city they call up Ansari and ask him for recommendations for the best places in town to eat (or avoid). He loves to check out local places wherever he visits. He gets suggestions and keeps lists from other equally "foodie" friends. His fast food of choice is Shake Shack, but he's always ready to try a new burger. He loves food so much that, in the *Dangerously Delicious* DVD, he listed the names of the restaurants where he ate when he was touring that material.

complain when they don't get to hear their favorite jokes when he's touring with mostly new material, but Ansari thinks that in reality they'd get sick of all the old jokes.

Even fans like his *Parks and Recreation* director Jason Woliner concede that Ansari has a challenge: if he's going to follow in the footsteps of his role

He doesn't want to get into a rut by always making rapper jokes, but so long as R. Kelly keeps doing "amazing things," Ansari will keep talking about it.

models, he has to keep his topics and jokes fresh. "Hopefully he won't lose that wonder at falling into these very strange situations," Woliner told Dave Itzkoff. That might sound like it means resisting the temptation to make jokes about R. Kelly. But does it? Ansari ultimately decided that, as he told Itzkoff, "R. Kelly keeps doing amazing things. I'd be failing at my job if I didn't address them."

CHAPTER FOUR

Stylin' Stand Up: Ansari on Stage

Although he has what seems like an incredibly strenuous tour schedule of back-to-back shows, Ansari doesn't complain at all. First of all, stand up is what he loves to do most. Second, he doesn't have much to do on the day of a show until performance time, he says. Often, he spends the day checking out the town and looking for places to get some tasty food.

Special Delivery from Aziz

Ansari can be a ball of frenetic energy on stage. Jason Zinoman calls it "hyperactive showmanship and a high-pitched, rat-a-tat delivery." Amanda Dobbins describes Ansari's vocals as well: "Volume is important to Ansari's comedy, and he yells to communicate a wide range

He can be a high-energy presence on stage, but in person Ansari tends to be far more laid back and relaxed.

of feelings: Awe! Indignation! Tacos!" Nevertheless, Ansari is calm before he performs. In an article for *Billboard* magazine, he told George Gurley, "Yeah, well, that's the thing: Any high-energy comedian like [Dave] Chappelle or Chris Rock, they're generally, like, pretty low-key dudes," he says. "Like, that's the stage, that's how you're performing. But if I was like that in my regular conversation, it would be very annoying." In his later performances, such as at Madison Square Garden, the audience got a breather as Ansari went into more detailed, longer stories.

Some of the successes of Ansari's jokes rest purely on his delivery. Sometimes Ansari acts his stories out as he tells them, recreating an interaction between a couple or even personifying meat and vegetables, as he did at Madison Square Garden. Many of these routines would not translate to paper at all. They come to life with Ansari's acting. Not everyone feels that the connections Ansari makes in his jokes are cutting-edge, but his delivery is considered so funny and sincere that they work. He chooses everyday observations, but he delves into their details and makes them come alive as he acts them out.

At the same time, he juxtaposes impromptu audience interactions with stories that have become far more personal. He asks people how they met their partners, how long they'd been together before they tied the knot. And in a sense, Ansari realized he was doing inadvertent research. He found talking to people very helpful, especially when it came to subjects where he didn't have experience, such as online dating.

Venues Big and Small

In 2014, Ansari performed ten sold-out shows to crowds of 1,200 people each in the Wilbur Theatre, in Boston, Massachusetts, breaking a one-hundred-year record at the century-old venue. "This is the 10th show here at the same venue, and it's cool but it gets a little repetitive," he explained to Gurley.

Although he likes the new crowds each night, at the same time it feels a little strange to perform at the same place over and over.

Generally Ansari prefers to perform in the smaller spaces, where he can be more intimate and get to know the crowd. But when the opportunity to play at the famous Madison Square Garden, which seats eighteen thousand people, came about, he gave

Ansari performs at the Waldorf-Astoria. He prefers the intimacy of smaller venues, but he wasn't about to pass up the opportunity to makes jokes at Madison Square Garden!

it some serious thought. "There is something very insane and amazing about starting stand-up in New York City at the lowest rung—open-mike spots—and then many years later going to the other utmost, utmost extreme of playing Madison Square Garden," he admitted to Gurley. "I felt a sense of that when I did Carnegie Hall, but Madison Square Garden is another level." The offer to perform at New York's hugely famous largest venue was humbling.

This comedian went into his biggest show to date with a goal of making his performance stand out. He consulted a Madison Square Garden pro, who just happens to be a funny guy he's looked up to since high school: Chris Rock. It was Rock's idea for him to film his performance there. Knowing that performing in a stadium is very different than the smaller spaces he was used to, Ansari decided to get some experience doing his acts for large audiences. He also decided that most arena comedy shows didn't have an interesting setup. What he wanted was something "interesting but not distracting. I can't have crazy spectacles of lights or lasers shooting out during my jokes," he explained to Jesse David Fox. So Ansari went ahead and funded the extra costs required to use a special screen that would hang above him. A cameraperson filmed him—head to toe—without any cuts, so that the audience saw a "giant Aziz" above him. At other

ON TOPIC

When he creates a comedy special, Ansari likes to stick to a central theme. He told Dobbins, "I didn't want to have to do random bits. It would be like, Hold on a second... I know I'm talking about all this stuff about marriage, but let me take a breather to tell you this funny story about what happened when I went to Trader Joe's." So in his *Buried Alive* special he almost exclusively stuck to topics like marriage, having children, and meeting and dating new people. As he gets older and has more experiences, of course his topics have evolved.

festivals where multiple screens were used, he felt like the audience was staring at the screens instead of the performer, as though everyone got together to watch a movie. This technique, he hoped, would make the show more intimate.

Despite the immensity of the space in Madison Square Garden, as well as the thousands of people there and a dramatic introduction, Ansari treated it like a small theater. Interacting with such a huge crowd could be difficult, but Ansari still managed to engage directly with his audience. He picked a woman from the crowd, brought her up on stage, and got her to agree to let him read one of her text messages, all while keeping the audience rapt.

Funny Feminist

When he was interviewed on the *Late Show with David Letterman*, Ansari explained how his girl-friend, chef Courtney McBroom, has influenced him. "She's a big feminist. That made me think about those kinds of issues. I'm a feminist as well. Any feminists out here: clap if you're a feminist?'" After the audience responded, he addressed anyone

Courtney McBroom and Aziz Ansari got together in 2013. Dating McBroom has made him think and talk about feminist issues and the definition of feminism.

who didn't clap and said he doesn't believe them. Ansari reminded the audience that the definition of feminism is that men and women should have equal rights. He told David Letterman and his audience, "You're a feminist if you go to a Jay Z and Beyoncé concert, and you're not like, 'mmm, I feel like Beyoncé should get 23% less than Jay Z. Also, I don't think Beyoncé should have the right to vote, and why is Beyoncé singing and dancing? Shouldn't she make Jay a steak? I'm sure he's very tired after walking and rapping those two songs.'"

Ansari's Netflix special, *Aziz Ansari: Live at Madison Square Garden*, doesn't shy away from feminism and how clueless men can be about it. But he's not just tackling the topic for laughs. Sure, he's funny, but Ansari is very serious about the matter. As he told journalist Darla Murray, "When I asked, 'Raise your hand if you're a woman and you've been followed,' and all those women raised their hand, there were a lot of dudes who were like, 'What?! That's happening?' A lot of this stuff dudes are not aware of." Ansari explained that he had actually cut a bit from the special in which he asked the men in the audience to clap if they had been surprised by the women's response. Many men had clapped. These audience interactions made Ansari much more aware of the immensity of the issue.

Although Ansari is serious about speaking out for women, he admits it's not always easy. Once he found himself with a group of people and someone made a misogynistic comment. He was shocked. "I didn't like that that person said that, and I'm going to say something. So I said something…and as soon as I did other people were like, 'Yeah.' I think it's a good thing to say something. Maybe the next time that person is in a situation where they're going to make a remark like that, they'll think twice. If someone says something racist, you wouldn't let it slide. You'd probably say something, depending on the context of the situation."

Stereotypes and Controversy

Ansari's insatiable curiosity is evident in what is perhaps the most controversial section of *Buried Alive*, in which Ansari discusses "'his favorite racial stereotype ever': "Black men having explosive reactions to magic tricks," as Erik Adams put it in his article for the *A.V. Club* website. It leans heavily on jokes of the "white guys drive like this, black guys drive like this" variety, Adams notes, but it's so quirky that he pulls it off. Not only that, but the topic evolves into a "meta-commentary of such sweeping stereotypes" once Ansari suggests the world would be a better place if people reacted to unfamiliar things with the enthusiasm with which black men—in his telling, at least—respond to magicians. As an example, he pretends to be a homophobic person whose initial revulsion to gay people quickly fades into the realization that "any love and joy in the world's a beautiful thing."

Despite this well-known bit, Ansari doesn't rely heavily on stereotypes in his act. When other comedians subjected Ansari to what *Jezebel* writer Madeleine Davies called "a barrage of tired and lazy jokes made at the expense of his Indian heritage" during Comedy Central's roast of James Franco, Ansari couldn't help but notice how weak those jokes were. When his turn to speak came around, Ansari joked, "I think it's so cool that some of you guys were able to travel back in time to 1995 for those Indian jokes you did...Those stereotypes are so outdated, my god."

Rapping About Rappers

It's no secret that Ansari has been a huge fan of rap music since he was a teen when he used to watch rappers on MTV. Stories abound about how he is allegedly such great friends with the likes of rapper Kanye West that they hang out all the time. He admits that one time West invited him over to listen to some music he was working on. As he explained to Carrie Battan, "I like that music and took on that role by being a fan of those guys in the same way

Although Ansari is huge fan of rap music, the rampant rumors about how he hangs out with Kanye West all the time are indeed just rumors.

I'm really into food and have become friends with chefs." According to Ansari, he and West have only met a few times, but his joke exploded and was passed among so many people that it took on a life of its own.

Ansari's love of R&B and rap music and musicians comes up in many of his comedy routines. Kanye West heard one such performance and was so flattered that he invited Ansari to a party at his home. This turned into yet another comedy bit for Ansari's routines.

Sometimes Ansari simply recounts stories and interactions with rap's biggest stars and their music. Other times he satirizes them. You might expect that rappers' lavish lifestyles would be a fascinating topic, but Ansari often takes a more thoughtful and interesting approach. For example he delves into their focused commitment to technique. During an interview with Dave Itzkoff he refers to *The Carter*, a Lil Wayne documentary: "He says something that I thought was really funny. It's like: 'Repetition is the father of learning. I repeat, repetition is the father of learning'… Not to compare myself to Lil Wayne," he said, "but that's why I'm repeating my set three times tonight, to see if I can figure it out."

Ansari compares comics to rappers, too. He talks about how rappers always have a "cool" persona but comics don't play the cool guy, "They have a great sense of humor… There's just not a self-deprecating rapper; that wouldn't work," he told Terry Gross. "If you're a rapper and you're like, 'I saw this girl, but I was too scared'—that doesn't work for a rapper."

Culture Comedy

Sure, Ansari talks about his Indian heritage in his comedy, but he won't bring it up in his routines just for the sake of a cheap laugh. Ansari just doesn't emphasize this part of his life in his jokes. He is sometimes compared to Mindy Kaling, another Indian comedian who doesn't make too much of her background in her comedy. What he will do, however, is delve into the weird quirks of his life— regardless of whether or not they have anything to do with his culture—and bring them to light in a way that makes everyone laugh and think.

And for the record, Ansari's jokes are enjoying international popularity, based on Netflix records. Ansari's specials, such as *Buried Alive*, have been hits all around the world, regardless of language and culture. This kind of popularity is rather unusual among comedians.

Early on in his career, Ansari refused to play Indian IT (information technology) guys. After getting offers for these kinds of parts, he flat out told his agent that he'd never take a part where the jokes only worked because they relied on Indian culture. Finally, they stopped sending him those kinds of parts. If the opportunity arose, Ansari says he would be interested in working on a Tamil action movie, because he's enjoyed some Tamil films. He speaks the language a little and understands most of it.

The Look of Comedy

Ansari is just as concerned with the look of his specials as he is with the fine tailored suits he eventually started wearing when he performs. He made the switch to formal wear when he started performing in theaters. At first, he started doing it to stand out in a room full of jokesters wearing T-shirts and jeans, and to give a nod to the stereotype of the cheesy comedian in a bad suit. But now it's more natural. He told Kelefa Sanneh "Now, when I don't do it, it feels like I'm—not phoning it in, but it just feels more proper when I'm dressed up."

Ansari has also developed a keen eye for making his specials stand out visually. He says he didn't think too much about how his first two specials looked. When he filmed *Buried Alive*, he was focused on camera angles. When he prepared for his Madison Square Garden show, he decided he wanted it to look more like a film, not like a cable

Ansari performs for the WE HATE HURRICANES Comedy Benefit for AmeriCares in 2012, sporting a snappy suit. He started wearing suits when he began working in theaters.

comedy show. So he watched some Richard Pryor specials from the 1980s. His entrance into Madison Square Garden is a nod to Pryor, who also walks through the crowd in *Richard Pryor Live on the Sunset Strip*. Then he started talking to directors Dylan Southern and Will Lovelace. He'd seen their work with the music group LCD Soundsystem and liked it. Finally, he decided on an old movie theater look for the stage, with lightbulbs all along the edge of the stage and a curtain.

In the past, Ansari has toured his stand-up work between seasons of *Parks and Recreation* or movies. Although he enjoys working on movies, stand up is what he enjoys most.

Wit on the Web

Aziz Ansari joined the ranks of Twitter users in May 2007. By June 2015, his social media account had more than six million followers. In a lot of ways, Ansari is excited about the possibilities offered by the reach of the World Wide Web. He is encouraged at how the Internet has opened up opportunities for people in isolated places and given people who weren't in the spotlight in the past the ability to express themselves.

Twitter for Titters...and as a Tool

Ansari seems to have a blast with his Twitter account, making up plans with people he's never even met. According to his feed, as Ellen Gamerman reported, Ansari has "eaten brunch with the R&B band Boyz II Men, had sushi with *Blood Diamond* actor Djimon Hounsou and beaten World Wrestling Entertainment star John Cena in a push-up competition. None of this is true."

Head to the web to follow Aziz Ansari on Twitter, where he might live-tweet a movie or give restaurant recommendations. You can also check out his website at http://azizansari.com.

Sometimes Ansari turns to Twitter when he's bored, such as when he's on an airplane. Once he was on a very long flight and got an idea for a film he went on to call *Ghost Plane*. To amuse himself, he started tweeting his screenplay ideas. He had such a good time writing *Ghost Plane* that he asked Conan O'Brien to do a table read of the script on his show, *Late Night with Conan O'Brien*. O'Brien's cohost, Andy Richter, pitched in, too. Ansari played the "handsome Indian guy, Raj" while giving the 6-foot, 4-inch (1.9-meter) tall, redheaded comedian either female or screaming parts to read. When O'Brien questions why there would be ghosts on the airplane, Ansari responded in all seriousness, "Do you want to see a movie about ghosts on a plane or like a faulty latch?"

Although he has a lot of fun with social media, Ansari doesn't seem to take it very seriously. Some of his followers have even accused him of not being all that funny on Twitter. He has defended himself by pointing out that he'd rather focus on crafting the perfect hour of material for a new special than on overthinking every little thing he posts on Twitter.

Like many artists, Ansari uses Twitter as an instrument to reach out to his fans. Thanks to Twitter, he can reach out to millions of fans at any time. He explained to Jay Richardson, "I'm working on my new special and want to do this thing where I do small, impromptu 100-seater shows, work on it for an hour, an hour and a half. I can just tweet … an hour or two before, announce it and a couple of hundred people show up. I couldn't do that before Twitter." He also enjoys using his Twitter page to make restaurant recommendations.

When promoting his book, *Modern Romance*, Ansari used Twitter to talk about the book in a "Twitter rant" on May 28, 2015, including the following:

> *If you are single, you have problems like, "Why did this dude just text me 'Hey' and an emoji of a top hat?"*
>
> *Online dating is the biggest way people meet their spouses now, more than work, school, and friends COMBINED.*
>
> *Through online dating and beyond, single people now have an infinite number of – but how do you sort through infinite options?*
>
> *To learn about all of this, I teamed up with NYU sociologist Eric Klinenberg and we designed a massive research project.*
>
> *We also enlisted some of the best social scientists to help us understand and study all the facets of modern love and romance.*

COMEDY ON A BUDGET

In 2011, comic Louis C.K. did something unusual: He offered his wildly popular *Live at the Beacon Theater* show for only $5 on his website. Fans went crazy for this direct-release model and in less than two weeks the website had made $1 million! C.K. used part to pay for the special, part to give his staff bonuses, gave a large chunk to charity, and spent some on his family. In March that same year, Ansari's fans asked him to make his special available online, too. So he followed in C.K.'s footsteps and made his special *Dangerously Delicious* available to fans for $5 a download on his website. C.K., Ansari, and other comedians are on to something here. Obviously, this makes them money, but making their specials available in this way does something they feel is much more important. It gives them the creative freedom to produce what they want, without censors, time limitations, or advertising. Ansari went on to offer future specials to his fans this way as well.

Show Time Tech

Technology has shouldered its way into comedy shows, too, and Ansari feels like it's an intrusion for a few different reasons. He recently had to make a practice of announcing at the beginning of a show that he doesn't want anyone to record his performance. He isn't trying to be difficult or give the crowd a hard time. When he's working on a bit that gets put up on YouTube, the surprise of the joke or story is ruined for other people who haven't seen his current show yet. He also finds that the uploads are sometimes cut off in strange places and don't clearly convey the full story or joke. Then would-be audience members get the wrong impression of his

A few photos before a show is fine, but Ansari asks the audience to put their phones away for the performance.

work. Ansari will sometimes share a bit of his special or current tour routine on shows—such as *Late Night with Conan O'Brien*—so people get an idea of what he's doing and can see if they like it. However, Ansari gets to have a say in what gets distributed in those cases. Despite his opposition to the practice, Ansari never asks anyone to take down clips from past material or shows.

Taking a quick picture of a favorite celebrity like Ansari might not seem like a big deal, but, as he explained to Hardwick, "as a performer you don't want to perform for a room full of phones in your face." Ansari really wants to see the audience and see their faces light up (or if they don't) with laughter when his jokes reach them. Seeing the backs of cell phones and the eerie blue glow they cast doesn't help him determine whether or not he's connecting with the audience.

If the audience really wants photos, Ansari is willing to cooperate a bit. Before he begins his routine in earnest, he acts as though he's performing his stand-up routine and lets people take photos. And then he politely asks the people in the audience to put their phones and other devices away for the rest of the show. He finds that usually people are pretty cooperative.

GIVING COMEDIAN

Ansari can be serious when it comes to supporting causes he thinks are important. For example, he stills feels very strongly about his alma matter, South Carolina Governor's School for Science and Mathematics (GSSM). So much so that he performed seven sold-out shows to raise money for it in 2012. He explained to Susan Cohen in an article for *Charleston City Paper*, "Going to the school helped me grow in a myriad of ways, and I feel it's important for kids in South Carolina to have the opportunity to go there." All the money he raised in these shows went into a fund that supports the GSSM programs, such as a scientific research program (required of all students), as well as technology and scholarships.

In 2012, he loaned his talents to Oxfam, an organization that fights hunger and poverty. In a video called *Oxfam Unwrapped*, Ansari voiced the character of a goat to encourage people to make holiday donations to support Oxfam's cause. After the Boston Marathon bombings in 2014, he performed a benefit show at the Wilbur Theatre and donated the proceeds to victims of the bombing.

Also in 2012, Ansari took part in a benefit for an organization called Justin's Gift. This organization was created after fifteen-year-old Justin Aaberg took his own life when he could not escape verbal and physical abuse from some of his classmates because of his sexual

(continued on the next page)

(continued from the previous page)

orientation. His family and friends created Justin's Gift to help others who might be bullied for any reason. Within days of reading an article about Justin and other bullied classmates in *Rolling Stone* magazine, Ansari held an impromptu benefit. It sold out. Ansari was so pleased with the support from his show that he planned a second one in Los Angeles with comic stars Chelsea Peretti, Hannibal Buress, and Nick Kroll.

Offline Time

For all his Internet success, Ansari is trying to limit his own time on his smartphone, so sometimes he'll deliberately leave it at home when he goes out. He does this because he's concerned about what so much screen time is doing to his brain. He also uses special blocking software to prevent access to news blogs and websites such as Reddit, a news, social networking, and entertainment website. And in true character—he is always thorough—he even went to a hypnotist. As he explained to Amanda Dobbins, becoming less dependent on your smartphone is "like quitting smoking. But you always have a lit cigarette, and you have to smoke for work, and you have to do it to have a social life."

His concerns about electronic communication have worked their way into his stand-up material as well. At one point in his act he asks an audience member to let him check out her phone and reads her text messages, discussing frequency and punctuation with her. In another, he helps a young man compose his very first message to the girl he met that morning, even to the point of debating the number of question marks he should use. (Later, the young man let Ansari know that the girl said yes.)

In his Madison Square Garden show, Ansari talks about how he feels technology has essentially ruined humankind. He thinks in many ways it has made people rude and able to casually cancel plans at the last minute because it's so easy and impersonal to send a quick text instead of calling and talking to the person. Texting makes breaking off plans a lot less personal when you don't have to see someone's face or hear the disappointment in his or her voice.

Off the Job...Occasionally

Ansari loves his work so much he's been described as only loving to eat more than comedy. When he was given the choice of doing a movie—which many people consider a pretty cool option— on his hiatus from *Parks and Recreation*, Ansari said he'd rather stay in New York and hone his stand up or even

Aziz Ansari loves writing and performing stand-up comedy so much that he sometimes has to remind himself to take a break and go on vacation!

tour. Unless the film is really something he's into, Ansari told David Jesse Fox that stand up is "way more fun."

In spite of his insatiable desire to work all the time, Ansari does try to make himself take a break from stand up to live and have some experiences. Material comes from living and having life experiences that people can relate to, like dating and going out in *Buried Alive*. "Do things!" he tells Hardwick. "There's an infinite number of experiences in life that you haven't had."

Aziz Ansari is a relatively young comedian and some critics question whether he belongs on lists alongside legendary, long-time comics. But Ansari has made great strides for a minority who has only been on stage for a few years. Keep watching this guy, and keep laughing. Ansari plans to keep viewers on their toes. As he told Dave Itzkoff, he aims to keep his work exciting and excellent, and "keep changing people's expectations of what my bits are supposed to be." And with that plan in place, there's no telling what hilarious heights he'll reach.

Fact Sheet ON AZIZ ANSARI

Full name: Aziz Ishmael Ansari

Birthplace: Columbia, South Carolina

Birthdate: February 23, 1983

Parents: Shoukath and Fatima Ansari

High Schools Attended: Marlboro Academy in Bennettsville, South Carolina, and South Carolina Governor's School for Science and Mathematics (GSSM) in Hartsville, South Carolina

College Attended: New York University

Height: 5'6" (1.68 m) tall

Favorite television shows: *Breaking Bad, Mad Men, Curb Your Enthusiasm*, and *Louie*

Favorite restaurant: Zingerman's Deli, in Ann Arbor, Michigan

Favorite pizza in Los Angeles: Osteria Mozza

First music album bought: Michael Jackson's *Thriller*

Comedic Influences: Chris Rock, Patton Oswalt, and Louis C.K.

Career if he wasn't a comedian: A haberdasher, someone who works with men's suits

Funniest people he knows: His little brother and Amy Poehler

Fact Sheet ON AZIZ ANSARI'S WORK

Comedy Troupes

Upright Citizens Brigade
Human Giant

Comedy Specials

2010 *Intimate Moments for a Sensual Evening*
2012 *Dangerously Delicious*
2013 *Buried Alive*
2015 *Aziz Ansari: Live at Madison Square Garden*

Television Credits

2004 *Uncle Morty's Dub Shack*, "Didja Listen to My Demo?," MC Bricklayer
2005 *New York Noise*, "Aziz Ansari & Rob Huebel as Pitchfork's Editors," Thadius P. Scornburner
2005–2010 *Shutterbugs*, multiple episodes, Bill
2006 *Cheap Seats: Without Ron Parker*, "1991 Rose Bowl," Rosebowl Director
2007 *Flight of the Conchords*, "Drive By," Sinjay
2007–2008 *Human Giant*, multiple episodes, various characters
2008 *Worst Week*, "Pilot," Morgue Employee
2009 *Raaaaaaaandy!*, multiple episodes, Raaaaaaaandy
2009 Scrubs, multiple episodes, Ed
2009 *Reno 911!* , "Viacom Grinch" and "Getaway

Trailer," Resort Salesman #3/Insurance Representative

2007–2015 *Parks and Recreation*, multiple episodes, Tom Haverford

2010 *The Life & Times of Tim*, "Nagging Blonde/Tim and the Elephant," Gabe (voice)

2012– *Bob's Burgers*, multiple episodes, Darryl (voice)

2013 *Wander Over Yonder,* "The Little Guy," Westley (voice)

2013 *The League*, "The 8 Defensive Points of Hanukkah," Dr. Henry Rocha

2013 *Adventure Time*, "Be More," DMO (voice)

2013 *The Venture Bros., "What Color Is Your Cleansuit?,"* Martin (voice)

2015 *Kroll Show*, "Body Bouncers," Sly Dufrense

2015– *Master of None*, multiple episodes, Dev

Film Credits

2006 *School for Scoundrels*, Classmate

2008 *The Rocker*, Aziz

2009 *Observe and Report*, Saddamn

2009 *I Love You, Man*, Eugene

2009 *Funny People*, Randy

2010 *Get Him to the Greek*, Matty

2011 *30 Minutes or Less*, Chet

2011 *What's Your Number?*, Jay

2011 *Free Hugs*, Mike

2011 *Scrat's Continental Crack-Up: Part 2*, Squint (voice)
2012 *Ice Age: Continental Drift*, Squint (voice)
2012 *Cruel Summer,* Prisoner
2013 *This Is the End*, himself
2013 *Epic,* Mub (voice)
2014 *Date and Switch*, Marcus
2014 *Food Club*, Captain Ansari

Video Game Credits

2012 *Ice Age: Continental Drift—Arctic Games*, Squint (voice)

Music Video Appearances

2011 "Otis," by Jay Z and Kanye West

Books

2015 *Modern Romance*, published by Penguin Press

Critical Reviews

Aziz Ansari: Intimate Moments for a Sensual Evening

"Aziz Ansari is an enigma. With one look, you think he's a total nerd. However, his confidence and coolness spin that nerdiness into something envious for us regular guys. In the stand-up special, you get a chance to see Ansari as more human and less of the caricature he plays on the screen." — Kevin Carr, *7M Pictures*

Aziz Ansari: Dangerously Delicious

"Much of *Dangerously Delicious* deals with one of three topics: Ansari's fame, Ansari's troubles with girls, and race. With any number of other established comics, this kind of "I'm famous and it's hard!" material might grate, but Ansari's warm boyishness pulls it off, whether he's shaking his head at the practical application of obscure racial slurs or recounting how the people who recognize him in public are mostly dorks."—Austin L. Ray, *The Spittake*

Aziz Ansari: Buried Alive

"After a while, it feels like Ansari belabors the same points, and his extended riffs on the unlikelihood of meeting your soulmate get to be a little repetitive. At the same time, he's convincingly introspective about

the subject, even with his lengthy tangents about ghosts or how much black people love magic tricks. It's clear that Ansari has thought a lot about what it means to get married, to start a family, to knowingly take on all the trappings of a traditional life. He breaks it down so extensively that one of his strongest bits involves imagining how the idea of marriage would sound to someone who's never heard of it. At his best, Ansari offers a kind of deconstructionist perspective on a subject most people take for granted."
—Josh Bell, *The Spittake*, on the Netflix release

Aziz Ansari: Live at Madison Square Garden

"[Aziz Ansari] retains his effortless charisma and youthful exuberance even when talking about how horrible men are to women all of the time. He's a more fully rounded comic now, a wiser and braver performer whose material now matches his stature, and one who has grown comfortably into his role near the top of the current stand-up hierarchy."—Garret Martin, *Paste* magazine

Modern Romance

"Always-hilarious Aziz Ansari proves you can be smart and funny at the same time... I really learned stuff. Where was this book when I was 22 years

old?"—Steven Levitt, coauthor of Freakonomics
"*Modern Romance* is just like Aziz Ansari himself—
charming, thoughtful, reasonable, and able to distill
the madness of the world into something both sane
and wildly funny."—Dave Eggers

"The ever hip and funny comedian and *Parks and
Recreation* star embarks on a surprisingly insightful
exploration of the complex realities of dating today...
Ansari's eminently readable book is successful, in
part, because it not only lays out the history, evolu-
tion, and pitfalls of dating, it also offers sound advice
on how to actually win today's constantly shifting
game of love. Often hilarious, consistently informative, and unusually helpful."—*Kirkus Reviews*

"Ansari and Klinenberg elegantly capture the entirely
new ways that singles communicate, court, and find
love today. *Modern Romance* is a captivating read,
with deep insight into history, science, and culture,
and loads of wit and charm. Along the way, you may
even collect some valuable tips for finding a soul
mate."— Helen Fisher, Senior Research Fellow, The
Kinsey Institute

Timeline

1983 Aziz Ansari is born in Columbia, South Carolina, on February 23.

2000 Ansari heads to college at New York University, where he studies marketing. He starts performing at open-mike nights.

2004 Ansari graduates from NYU with a bachelor's degree in marketing.

2005 Ansari develops the sketch group *Human Giant*. He is named "Hot Standup" by *Rolling Stone* magazine in its Hot List. He wins award for Best Male Stand-Up at the Emerging Comics of New York. He is only twenty-two years old.

2006 Ansari wins the Jury Award for Best Stand-up at the U.S. Comedy Arts Festival in Aspen, Colorado.

2007 *Human Giant* is picked up by MTV based on the video shorts Ansari made with Rob Huebel, Paul Scheer, and director Jason Woliner.

2008 Ansari moves to Las Vegas, Nevada.

2009 Ansari joins the cast of *Parks and Recreation*.

2010 *Intimate Moments for a Sensual Evening*, Ansari's first special, is released. He hosts the MTV Movie Awards. Ansari live-tweets his reactions to the entire *Twilight* movie.

2011 *Paste* magazine names Ansari's *Parks and Recreation* character, Tom Haverford, tenth on its list of "20 Best TV Characters of the Year." Ansari plays Chet, his first major motion picture role, in *30 Minutes or Less*.

2012 Ansari releases *Dangerously Delicious* through his own website.

2013 *Buried Alive* is released on Netflix.

2013 Ansari records a 12 inch (30 centimeter) vinyl album on the Third Man Records label in cooperation with Comedy Central. It features his *Dangerously Delicious* special.

2014 On December 12, Ansari receives *Variety* magazine's Power of Comedy Award.

2015 *The Aziz Ansari: Live at Madison Square Garden* special comes out. Ansari's first book, *Modern Romance: An Investigation*, is published.

Glossary

academic A person who teaches or does research at a college or university.

analysis Studying the details of something to get a better understanding of it.

arch Purposefully or exaggeratedly joking or teasing.

atheist One who does not believe in any god.

context The words or facts surrounding a specific statement or event that explain how that event or statement fits into a larger picture.

crossover The practice of attaining success in a different area or form.

emcee Short for master of ceremonies.

encore An extra performance at the end of a concert or show, usually at the request of the audience.

feminism The advocacy of equal rights for women.

gastroenterologist A doctor who deals with stomach and intestinal disorders.

homophobic Afraid of or opposed to people who are lesbian, gay, bisexual, or transgender.

hone To make sharper, efficient, or to improve.

impromptu Executed without prior planning, arrangement, or preparation.

improvise To make something, especially a performance, up as you go along.

intern A student, usually advanced, who works with an experienced worker to gain on-the-job experience.

juxtapose To view or place two things close together for the purpose of contrast.

marketing Endorsing or selling, which can include research and advertising, products or services.

misogynistic Showing or motivated by a hatred for women.

Muslim Following the religion of Islam, which considers Muhammad the prophet.

open mike A time at a club when people are invited to perform, usually comedy or music.

pertinent Relevant to the matter being discussed.

pilot A test episode of a television program that is aired to gauge how popular it might be.

premiere The very first performance of something, such as a play, comedy special, television show, or movie.

premise The foundation for a work or theory.

pseudonym A made-up name, sometimes used to maintain someone's privacy.

psychopath Someone suffering from a mental disorder, especially with violent or abnormal behavior.

screenplay A movie script, which usually includes directions for actors and scenes.

sexting Sending texts and pictures of a sexual nature.

short A short film (rather than a feature film).

sketch A short, funny performance or play that is usually only one scene in a comedy show.

sociologist A person who studies human society.

stand up A comedian who performs jokes by standing in front of a live audience, or comedy that is performed this way.

Tamil Referring to a person who lives in or comes from southern India and Sri Lanka.

troupe A group of entertainers who travel to different venues to perform.

venue The place where an event, such as a concert or sporting event, occurs.

For More Information

Canadian Comedy Foundation for Excellence
500c-720 Bathurst Street
Toronto, ON M5S 2R4
Canada
Website: http://www.canadiancomedy.ca
The Canadian Comedy Foundation for Excellence is
a nonprofit organization promotes Canadian
comedy all around the world.

Comedy Exchange Association (CXA)
4006 Gulfview
Rowlett, TX 75088
Attention: George Gimarc
(214) 228-5535
Website: http://www.mycomedyexchange.com
The Comedy Exchange Association fights for the
rights of comedians. It was created "to collect
performance royalties for comedians (who
perform their own material) and other comedic
writers whose recorded works are used on
AM / FM and other terrestrial radio
broadcasting."

International Society for Humor Studies (ISHS)
Martin Lampert, Executive Secretary
Holy Names University
Oakland, CA 94619
(510) 436-1532
Website: https://www.hnu.edu/ishs

The ISHS strives to promote scholarly research about humor. They publish a quarterly journal known as *Humor: International Journal of Humor Research* and host an international conference annually.

Justin's Gift
PO Box 542
Anoka, MN 55303
(763) 220-0153
Website: http://www.justinsgift.org
Justin's Gift is an organization that seeks to offer a safe, bully-free area where all kids can be comfortable and be themselves.

National Association of Comedians
60 3rd Avenue, Suite 597
Long Branch, NJ 07740
(732) 735-4292
Website: http://www.nacomedy.com
The National Association of Comedians provides seminars, education, and more. It offers benefits for comedians, comedy clubs, and others in the comedy business.

Oxfam America
226 Causeway Street, 5th Floor
Boston, MA 02114
(800) 776-9326

Website: http://www.oxfamamerica.org
Oxfam America strives to fight injustices such as
        hunger and poverty. It cooperates with seven-
        teen other members of International Oxfam,
        working in more than ninety countries.

Winnipeg Comedy Festival
The Gas Station Arts Centre
445 River Avenue
Winnipeg, MB R3L 0C3
Canada
(204) 284-9477
Website: http://www.winnipegcomedyfestival.com
The Winnipeg Comedy Festival is an annual festival
        of all things funny and provides year-round
        laughs with workshops, tours, television broad-
        casts, and more.

Websites

Because of the changing nature of Internet links,
Rosen Publishing has developed an online list of
websites related to the subject of this book. This site
is updated regularly. Please use this link to access
the list:

http://www.rosenlinks.com/COMEDY/Ansari

For Further Reading

Ansari, Aziz, and Eric Klinenberg. *Modern Romance: An Investigation*. New York, NY: Penguin Books, 2015.

Apatow, Judd. *Sick in the Head: Conversations About Life and Comedy*. New York, NY: Random House, 2015.

Besser, Matt, Ian Roberts, and Matt Walsh. *The Upright Citizens Brigade Comedy Improvisation Manual.* New York, NY: Comedy Council of Nicea, 2013.

Cleese, John. *So Anyway…* New York, NY: Crown Archetype, 2014.

Dean, Greg. *Step by Step to Stand-up Comedy*. Los Gatos, CA: Silverlake eBooks 2011. Kindle ed.

DeGeneres, Ellen. *Seriously—I'm Kidding.* New York, NY: Grand Central, 2011.

Drach, Rachel. *Girl Walks into a Bar…: Comedy Calamities, Dating Disasters, and a Midlife Miracle*. New York, NY: Gotham Books, 2012.

Fey, Tina. *Bossypants.* New York, NY: Little, Brown and Co., 2011.

Gaffigan, Jim. *Dad Is Fat*. New York, NY: Crown Archetype, 2013.

Gaffigan, Jim. *Food: A Love Story*. New York, NY: Crown Archetype, 2014.

Harris, Neil Patrick. *Neil Patrick Harris: Choose Your Own Autobiography*. New York, NY: Crown Archetype, 2014.

Hollander, Barbara Gottfried. *Ellen DeGeneres: TV's Funniest Host*. New York, NY: Rosen Publishing Group, 2015.

Hyperion. *Pawnee: The Greatest Town in America*. New York, NY: Hyperion, 2011.

Kaling, Mindy. *Is Everyone Hanging Out Without Me? (and Other Concerns)*. New York, NY: Crown Archetype, 2011.

Kaplan, Steve. *The Hidden Tools of Comedy: The Serious Business of Being Funny. Studio City*, CA: Michael Wiese Productions, 2013.

Libera, Anne. *The Second City Almanac of Improvisation*. Evanston, IL: Northwestern University Press, 2004.

Mandvi, Aasif. *No Man's Land*. San Francisco, CA: Chronicle Books, 2014.

Nayyar, Kunal. *Yes, My Accent Is Real: And Some Other Things I Haven't Told You*. New York, NY: Atria Publishing, 2015.

Offerman, Nick. *Paddle Your Own Canoe: One Man's Fundamentals for Delicious Living*. New York, NY: Dutton, 2014.

Poehler, Amy. *Yes Please*. New York, NY: Dey Street Books, 2014.

Sacks, Mike. *Poking a Dead Frog: Conversations With Today's Top Comedy Writers*. New York, NY: Penguin Books, 2014.

Sedaris, David. *Let's Explore Diabetes With Owls*. New York, NY: Little, Brown and Company, 2013.

Schuman, Michael A. *Tina Fey: TV Comedy Superstar (People to Know Today)*. Berkeley Heights, NJ: Enslow Publishing, 2011.

Short, Martin, and David Kamp. *I Must Say: My Life as a Humble Comedy Legend*. New York, NY: Harper, 2014.

Bibliography

Adam, Erik. "Aziz Ansari Becomes the Malcolm Gladwell of Stand-up Comedy. (And That's a Good Thing)." *A.V. Club*, November 1, 2013. Retrieved April 25, 2015 (http://www.avclub.com/review/emaziz-ansari-buried-aliveem-105061).

Alfuso, Renée. "Class Clowns." Retrieved May 26, 2015 (https://www.nyu.edu/alumni.magazine/issue18/18_FEA_ClassClowns.html).

Ansari, Aziz. Aziz Ansari Official Twitter Account. Retrieved June 2, 2015 (https://twitter.com/azizansari).

Ansari, Aziz. *Modern Romance*. 2015. Retrieved May 18, 2015 (http://book.azizansari.com/).

Ansari, Aziz. "Modern Romantics," Reddit.com. Retrieved May 18, 2015 (http://www.reddit.com/r/modernromantics/).

Battan, Carrie. "Aziz Ansari." *Pitchfork,* July 23, 2012. Retrieved April 13, 2015 (http://pitchfork.com/features/interviews/8894-aziz-ansari/).

Blackbook. "Human Giant's Aziz Ansari Takes Our Pop Quiz." *Blackbook*, January 9, 2009. Retrieved May 2, 2015 (http://www.bbook.com/human-giants-aziz-ansari-takes-our-pop-quiz/).

Cohen, Ian. "Aziz Ansari: Intimate Moments for a Sensual Evening." *Pitchfork*, January 20, 2010. Retrieved May 28, 2015 (http://pitchfork.com/reviews/albums/13832-intimate-moments-for-a-sensual-evening/).

Cohen, Susan. "Aziz Ansari Drops Science for Stand-up: Class Clown." *Charleston City Paper*, February 1, 2012. Retrieved April 15, 2015 (http://www.charlestoncitypaper.com/charleston/aziz-ansari-drops-science-for-stand-up/Content?oid=4007843).

Czajkowski, Elise. "Talking to Aziz Ansari About His New Special, 'Parks and Rec,' and Why He Prefers Standup to Films." *Splitsider,* October 31, 2013. Retrieved May 28, 2015 (http://splitsider.com/2013/10/talking-to-aziz-ansari-about-his-new-special-parks-and-rec-and-why-he-prefers-standup-to-films/).

Davies, Madeleine. "Watch Aziz Ansari Lay Waste to the Lazy Racism of His Fellow Comedians." *Jezebel*, September 5, 2013. Retrieved August 19, 2015 (http://jezebel.com/watch-aziz-ansari-lay-waste-to-the-lazy-racism-of-his-f-1258432112).

Dobbins, Amanda. "Aziz Ansari's Romantic Period: The Comedian on Relationships, Maturity, and His New Stand-Up Special." Vulture, October 20, 2013. Retrieved April 21, 2015 (http://www.vulture.com/2013/10/aziz-ansari-on-buried-alive.html).

Fox, Jesse David. "Aziz Ansari on Playing Madison Square Garden and the Last Season of *Parks and Recreation*." Vulture, October 8, 2014. Retrieved April 23, 2015 (http://www.vulture.com/2014/10/aziz-ansari-on-playing-madison-square-garden.html).

Friedman, Megan. "Aziz Ansari Explains Why He Is a Feminist With a Beyoncé Anecdote." *Cosmopolitan*, October 7, 2014. Retrieved April 21, 2015 (http://www.cosmopolitan.com/entertainment/tv/news/a31864/aziz-ansari-feminist-beyonce/).

Gamerman, Ellen. "The Rise of the Likable Jerk." *Wall Street Journal*, March 27, 2009. Retrieved May 2, 2015 (http://www.wsj.com/articles/SB123810831170052517).

Gross, Terri. "Aziz Ansari's Latest Is 'Dangerously Delicious'." *Fresh Air*, April 2, 2012. Retrieved April 16, 2015 (http://www.npr.org/2012/04/02/

149392896/aziz-ansaris-latest-is-dangerously-delicious).

Groth, Aimee. "Aziz Ansari Got His Start While At NYU Stern." *Business Insider*, August 14, 2011. Retrieved May 2, 2015 (http://www.businessinsider.com/aziz-ansari-nyu-stern-2011-8).

Haglage, Abby. *"Parks and Recreation*'s Aziz Ansari Is 30 Years Old and Writing a Book About Modern Love." *Daily Beast*, November 12, 2013. Retrieved May 3, 2015 (http://www.thedailybeast.com/articles/2013/11/12/parks-and-recreation-s-aziz-ansari-is-30-years-old-and-writing-a-book-about-modern-love.html).

Hardwick, Chris. "Nerdist Podcast: Aziz Ansari." *Nerdist*, November 11, 2013. Retrieved April 25, 2015 (http://nerdist.com/nerdist-podcast-aziz-ansari/).

Hundley, Jessica. "Aziz Ansari Interview." *AskMen*. Retrieved April 29, 2015 (http://www.askmen.com/celebs/interview_300/382_aziz-ansari-interview.html).

Itzkoff, Dave. "Feeding the Comedy Beast Without Serving Leftovers." *New York Times*, June 3, 2010. Retrieved April 25, 2015 (http://www.

nytimes.com/2010/06/04/arts/television/04aziz.
html?_r=0).

Itzkoff, Dave. "A Young Comic Joins an Exclusive
Club." *New York Times*, October 3, 2014.
Retrieved May 13, 2015 (http://www.nytimes.
com/2014/10/05/arts/television/aziz-ansari-
prepares-for-madison-square-garden.html?_r=1).

Murray, Darla. "A Heart-to-Heart About Feminism
With Aziz Ansari." *Cosmopolitan*, March 10,
2015. Retrieved April 21, 2015 (http://www.
cosmopolitan.com/entertainment/celebs/q-
and-a/a37545/aziz-ansari-feminism-interview/).

Richardson, Jay. "'All the Best Comics Have a
Tremendous Work Ethic': Q&A with Parks &
Rec's Aziz Ansari." *Chortle*, June 7, 2013.
Retrieved May 3, 2015 (http://www.chortle.
co.uk/interviews/2013/06/07/18051/all_the_
best_comics_have_a_tremendous_work_ethic).

Robinson, Melia. "Aziz Ansari Asked Reddit Users
Personal Questions About Dating In The Digital
Age — And The Responses Were Amazing."
Business Insider, March 5, 2013. Retrieved May
13, 2015 (http://www.businessinsider.com/
aziz-ansari-modern-romantics-subreddit-2014-3).

Robinson, Melia. "9 Amazing Stories from the Set of 'Parks and Recreation.'" *Business Insider,* February 18, 2015. Retrieved May 2, 2015 (http://www.businessinsider.com/parks-and-recreation-behind-the-scenes-stories-2015-2).

Ryan, Kyle. "Aziz Ansari: Intimate Moments For A Sensual Evening." *A.V. Club*, February 3, 2010. Retrieved May 26, 2015 (http://www.avclub.com/review/aziz-ansari-intimate-moments-for-a-sensual-evening-37812).

Sanneh, Kelefa. "Funny Person." *The New Yorker,* November 1, 2010. Retrieved April 15, 2015 (http://www.newyorker.com/magazine/2010/11/01/funny-person).

Shepherd, Julianne Escobedo. *"Aziz Ansari's New Girlfriend Turned Him Into a Feminist."* Jezebel, October 7, 2014. Retrieved April 13, 2015 (http://jezebel.com/aziz-ansaris-new-girlfriend-turned-him-into-a-feminist-1643321094).

Sims, David. "Aziz Ansari Catches Up With His Fame at Madison Square Garden." *Atlantic*, March 7, 2015. Retrieved April 23, 2015 (http://www.theatlantic.com/entertainment/archive/2015/03/aziz-ansari-catches-up-with-his-fame-at-madison-square-garden/387151/).

TeamCoco. "Aziz Ansari's Twitter Screenplay." *Late Night with Conan O'Brien*, March 3, 2015. Retrieved May 3, 2015 (http://teamcoco.com/video/aziz-ansari-twitter-screenplay).

Weisman, Aly. "20 Things You Didn't Know About Aziz Ansari." *Business Insider*, January 25, 2012. Retrieved May 2, 2015 (http://www.businessinsider.com/20-things-you-didnt-know-about-aziz-ansari-2012-1?op=1).

Zinoman, Jason. "In a Big House, but Playing It Small." *New York Times*, October 10, 2014. Retrieved May 1, 2015 (http://www.nytimes.com/2014/10/11/arts/aziz-ansari-plays-madison-square-garden.html?_r=3).

Index

About the Author

Heather Moore Niver has written more than two dozen books for children from second through twelfth grades. Among her titles are *All About the Author: Veronica Roth, Britannica Beginner Biographies: Malala Yousafzai, and Heroes of Black History: Sojourner Truth*. She laughs, writes, and edits in New York State.

Phot Credits